UP & DOWN

Explore the world from above and below!

Illustrated by WENJIA TANG

What is the world like above and below?

Let's go on an adventure and find out!

VICTION VICTION

Poster

Stairs

Pipe

Map

Escalator

Lift

Bench

Litter Bin

Vending
Machine

Platform

Train

Handles

Tracks

4
2nd AVE

Train
Driver

Passengers

AT THE
Station

When was the last time
you travelled by train?

Periodic Table

Shelves

Plant Specimens

Scientist

Safety Goggles

Mask

Lab Coat

Solution

Flasks

Burner

Beakers

Microscope

IN THE

laboratory

Be careful – experiments
can be exciting but dangerous!

Test Tubes

Dropper

Petri Dish

Parrot

Sloth

Snake

Leaves

Waterfall

Frog

Grasshopper

Monkey

Butterflies

Fern

Crocodile

Chameleon

IN THE
Rainforest

Which of these wild creatures
would you like to meet?

AT THE
Cottage

Roses

Chimney

Cottage

Picket Fence

Window

Squirrel

Acorn

Mushrooms

Watering Can

Path

Lavender

Hen

Sunflowers

Irises

Chicks

Soil

Scorpion

Earthworm

Roots

Burrow

Fox

Rabbit

Berries

Field Mouse

Ants

Spider

UNDER THE
garden

Some creatures can dig
holes that go very deep!

Stars

Watch Tower

Castle

Moon

Hills

Fairy

Gate

Prince

Guard

Princess

Unicorn

Pine Trees

Witch

Broomstick

Fog

AT THE
Castle

IN THE
Dungeon

Would you keep a secret pet dragon?

Oil Lamp

Pillar

Torch

Brick Wall

Sword

Dragon

Necklace

Gold Bars

Coins

Crystals

Rings

Diamond

Trophy

Treasure Chest

Bats

Bull

Spear

Deer

Cave Paintings

Cavewoman

Pot

Fossil

Caveman

Skewer

Fire

Firepit

Arrows

Quiver

Bow

IN THE
Cave

Once upon a time, people
lived in caves – not houses!

A party is full of people having fun!

AT THE
Poolside

String Lights

Curtains

Server

Deck Chairs

Swimming Pool

Buffet Table

Tray

Float

Party Guests

Grill

Lamp

Painting

Wine Cellar

Television

Peacock
Feathers

Dartboard

Wine

Vase

Bar

Stool

Billiard Balls

Cue Stick

Rug

Billiard Table

IN THE
Den

Window Display

Café

Fast Food Restaurant

Canopy

Boutique

Burger

Mannequins

Glass Barrier

Drapes

Shopper

Fountain

Toy Store

Supermarket

Shopping Bags

Basket

AT THE
Mall

In the Car Park

Safety Mirror

Exit Sign

EXIT

Parking Space

Van

C

D D D

Corner Protector

Fire Hydrant

Helmet

Headlamp

Driver

Parking Block

Tyre

Directional Arrow

Motorcycle

Look out for cars and motorcycles when you are walking!

UNDER THE Ice

Penguin

Killer Whale

Shrimp

Narwhal

Tusk

Chain

Lion's Mane Jellyfish

Arctic Cod

Squid

Anchor

Seabed

Beluga Whale

IN THE Desert

It can get really hot, dry, and dusty here!

Owl

Cliffs

Acacia Tree

Camels

Fennec Fox

Chuckwalla

Coyote

Tortoise

Prickly Pear

Aloe

Bull Skull

Truck

Explorer

Monitor Lizard

Rattlesnake

Barrel Cactus

ON THE *Mountain*

Hot Air Balloon

Summit

Aeroplane

Fireworks

Sailboat

Lake

Bridge

Hiker

Hiking Trail

Cherry Blossom Tree

Cranes

Willow Tree

ON THE
Upper Decks

Helicopter

Ship Funnel

Sundeck

Diving Board

Floating Mat

Sun Umbrellas

Helipad

Changing Rooms

Sunlounger

Sunbather

Lifebuoy

Lifeboat

Portholes

Chandelier

Captain
Control Room

Card Game

Casino

Slot Machines

Stage

Cabins

Seats

Theatre

Engine Room

Engineer

Waves

Cruise ships are a great way to travel by sea!

IN THE
lower Decks

IN THE Tomb

Zombie

Ghost

Coffin

Tomb Raider

Skull

Urn

Rosary

Offerings

Skeleton

Mummy

Cobweb

Sarcophagus

Bones

Mummy

In the future, people could be living on new planets!

Laptop

Socket

Switches

Bunk Bed

Ladder

Bookcase

Control Screen

Heater

Paddle

Pod Chair

Coffee Table

Robot

Table Tennis

IN THE

living
Quarters

Bees

Beehive

Honey

Python

Woodpecker

Caterpillar

Tree Hollow

Tree Trunk

Moth

Ladybird

Toadstools

Letterbox

Toad

IN THE

Woods

Would you live in a house
that is in a tree?

Mirror

Wax

Candle

Dried Herbs

Crystal Ball

Wand

Powder

Witch

Potion

Fireplace

Pumpkin

Cauldron

Tarot Cards

Hourglass

Spell Book

IN THE *lair*

IN THE
Museum

Artwork

Frame

Artefact

Painter

Easel

Docent

Statue

Archway

Sculpture

Display Case

Pedestal

Sketch Book

Visitors

Wheelchair

Label

Menu Board

Paper Cups

Cashier

Juices

Cake

Fresh Fruits

Entrées

Counter

Bread

Cupcakes

Tablecloth

Dining Chair

Dining Table

AT THE
café

Looking at art all day
can make you very hungry!

Basketball Hoop

Players

Bleachers

Spectators

Washroom

Volleyball Net

Stationary Bicycle

Trainer

Treadmill

Coach

Exercise Mat

Dumbbells

IN THE
Gym

Which sport would you like to play?

10 10 10

Onion

Shallots

Radish

Carrot

Ginger

White Radish

Garlic

Parsnip

Beets

Potatoes

Taro

In the Soil

Which of these foods have you eaten?

Cherub

Dove

Rainbow

God

Halo

Violin

Flute

Angel

Lyre

Trumpet

Wings

IN

heaven

What song do you think
the angels are playing?